DISASTER ALERT!

Written by
Christine Taylor-Butler

Acknowledgments

The publisher would like to thank the following for their kind permission to reproduce their photographs: (Key: b-bottom; c-center; l-left; r-right; t-top) **Alamy Images:** Adrian Sherratt 11t, Andrew Johns Photography 14–15, Bjarki Reyr EYJ 24, Chris Howes / Wild Places Photography 17t, Christine Osborne Pictures 30b, Gene Rhoden 4–5, imageBROKER 21t, Jennifer Hart 29t, keith morris 14c, Kraig Lieb 10–11, Rafael Ben-Ari 27t, Randy Green 20–21, Stocktrek Images, Inc. 23b, 26, Westend61 GmbH 22b, 22–23t, William Caram 28b, Xinhua 28–29, ZUMA Press, Inc 5, 18; **Getty Images:** AFP / AFP 17b, 19b, ANDREW YATES / AFP 12, Christopher Furlong 13, HALLDOR KOLBEINS / AFP 27b, J. B. Spector / Museum of Science and Industry, Chicago 7cr, Jeff Hutchens 6–7t, JIJI PRESS / AFP 25, Joe Raedle 8cr, Julie Denesha 8, Red Huber / Orlando Sentinel / MCT via 19t, Robert Cianflone 31, SAEED KHAN / AFP 30t; **Shutterstock.com:** auremar 15b, f-f-f-f. 9bc, Minerva Studio 9b, Serg64 9tc

Cover images: *Front:* **Alamy Images:** Stocktrek Images, Inc.; *Back:* **Alamy Images:** Westend61 GmbH

All other images © Pearson Education

Every effort has been made to trace the copyright holders and we apologize in advance for any unintentional omissions. We would be pleased to insert the appropriate acknowledgment in any subsequent edition of this publication.

PEARSON

ISBN-13: 978-0-328-83283-5
ISBN-10: 0-328-83283-9

5 6 7   18 17 16

Contents

Tornadoes   4

Floods   10

Sinkholes   16

Volcanoes   22

Bushfires   28

Glossary and Index   32

Tornadoes

What Is a Tornado?

Tornadoes are the result of rotating thunderstorms. They form when warm air mixes with cold air and dry air. This creates a violent storm called a supercell. If the conditions are right, a supercell can produce a tornado without warning.

Tornadoes are dangerous because they move very fast. The average speed of a tornado moving along the ground is 30 miles per hour. Wind inside a tornado can reach speeds of more than 200 miles per hour. Most tornadoes occur in the United States. Tornadoes can last from several seconds to over an hour.

REAL LIFE

May 22, 2011
One of the biggest tornadoes ever recorded hit the town of Joplin, Missouri. The strong winds destroyed the town.

Studying Tornadoes

Scientists who study the weather are called meteorologists. They send out alerts when dangerous weather is spotted. Once a tornado is spotted, people have to find shelter immediately.

Meteorologists use a scale to measure tornadoes. The scale measures the strength of the storm. An EF0 is the weakest tornado. An EF5 is the strongest.

60–85 mph	*86–110 mph*	*111–135 mph*
EF0 **Light Damage**	**EF1** **Moderate Damage**	**EF2** **Considerable Damage**

Some roofs are damaged; branches are broken off trees.	Parts of roofs are peeled off; windows are broken; some tree trunks are snapped.	Roofs are torn off; large trees are uprooted; mobile homes are destroyed.

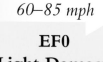
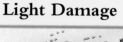

Job Profile

Storm chasers follow severe weather. They carry special equipment called probes. Probes are placed in the path of the storms. The probes measure wind speed and direction. They also measure temperature, humidity, and air pressure. This information is stored in a black box.

probe

136–165 mph	166–200 mph	Over 200 mph
EF3 **Severe Damage**	**EF4** **Devastating Damage**	**EF5** **Incredible Damage**
	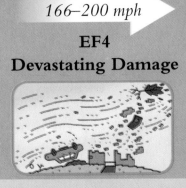	
Small buildings are destroyed; roofs and some walls are torn off well-built houses.	Well-built houses are destroyed; large objects are lifted into the air; cars are blown around.	Cars are lifted into the air; well-built houses are flattened and swept away.

Surviving a Tornado

This dog was rescued after a tornado struck Oklahoma City.

After a tornado, emergency workers look for survivors. They use specially-trained dogs to help them. People are taken to the hospital. Pets are taken to a shelter.

Tornadoes often break power lines and destroy buildings. After a tornado, power must be restored. Damaged buildings must be cleared away. It can take years to fix all the damage.

How to Survive

It's important to have the correct equipment and be prepared! When a tornado strikes:

- Have a flashlight and batteries ready.

- Stay away from windows.

- Find shelter underground.

- If you can't go underground, hide under a staircase.

- Protect yourself from flying objects.

DID YOU KNOW?

Waterspouts are tornadoes that form over water.

Floods

Why Do Floods Happen?

Floods usually happen when there is too much rain. The ground cannot absorb the water, and riverbanks overflow. In coastal areas, strong winds and high tides can cause floods.

In cities, heavy rain can cause drains to overflow. The water spills into streets and houses. Sometimes floods last a few hours. Sometimes it can take weeks for the water to go away.

REAL LIFE

July 20, 2007
Heavy rain hit the
town of Tewkesbury,
Gloucestershire, England.
Two months' worth of rain
fell in one day. Almost
50,000 homes lost electricity.
The rivers overflowed. Thousands of
homes were under water. There was
no drinking water for seventeen days.
The cost of fixing the damages in
Gloucestershire was $80 million.

Surviving a Flood

Floods can destroy roads and highways. Strong currents carry away houses and cars. Floodwaters can make tap water undrinkable and dangerous.

Power and phone service may be cut off for weeks. People are often trapped in their homes. Boats and helicopters are used to rescue them. Rescue workers search for lost pets too.

How to Survive

When flood warnings are issued:

- Move to higher ground.

- Gather canned food and drinking water.

- Don't cross deep water by foot or car.

- Turn off electrical items.

- Use a battery-powered radio to listen for warnings and information.

- Fill sinks and bathtubs with clean water.

Fixing the Damage

pumps

Cleaning up a flood is a big job. Pumps are used to carry water away from the town. Once the water is gone, people have to clean their houses. Furniture and other belongings are often ruined.

Job Profile

Electricians help restore power after a flood. It can be a dangerous job. Electricians must find safe ways to replace the power lines without getting hurt.

Sinkholes

What Are Sinkholes?

Sinkholes are found all over the world. They happen when water dissolves rock under the ground.
This makes a hole in the rock that soil can slip into.
Eventually the top of the land falls into the hole.

How Is a Sinkhole Formed?

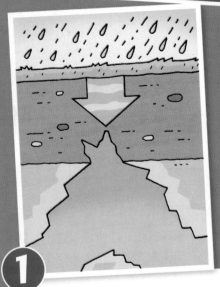

1 Water dissolves rock under the ground.

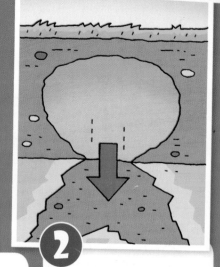

2 Soil slips into the hole in the rock.

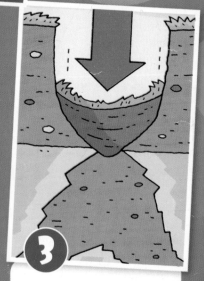

3 Land at the top falls into the hole.

Some sinkholes are made when underground pipes leak. Water from the pipes weakens the ground. Hidden underground caves can cause sinkholes too. The land above falls into the cave. This leaves a hole.

More than one million bats live in this sinkhole in Rocksprings, Texas.

This sinkhole appeared suddenly in Beijing, China.

Dangerous Sinkholes

Most sinkholes occur over time. Some, however, collapse quickly and without warning. Some sinkholes are a few feet wide. Others are large enough to swallow a building!

REAL LIFE

August 12, 2013

A sinkhole opened in Clermont, Florida. The windows began to pop out of a building. People ran for their lives. Soon after, the building fell into the hole.

Job Profile

Firefighters and emergency workers rush to rescue people from sinkholes. They bring ropes, ladders, or cranes to lift people from the hole. They ask other people to leave the area. There is no way to know if the hole will get bigger while they work.

Useful Sinkholes

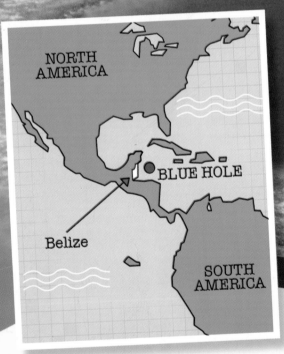

NORTH AMERICA

BLUE HOLE

Belize

SOUTH AMERICA

Not all sinkholes are dangerous. Some sinkholes allow scientists to explore places that are normally difficult to reach. For instance, the Blue Hole is a sinkhole under the sea near the coast of Belize. It formed thousands of years ago. Now it is a habitat for many animals.

limestone

DID YOU KNOW?

Limestone and gypsum are types of porous rock. This means they contain holes. These rocks can be dissolved by water. Many sinkholes are formed from these types of rocks.

Volcanoes

What Is a Volcano?

A volcano is a large opening in Earth's surface. It acts like a vent for Earth's heat and gases. Beneath Earth's surface, pressure and heat build up. This melts the rock and minerals. The molten hot rock is called magma. Magma escapes to the surface when a volcano erupts. When magma flows out of a volcano, it is called lava. Lava is dangerously hot.

Most volcanoes form over thousands of years.

lava

DID YOU KNOW?

- Jupiter's moon Io has more active volcanoes than Earth.
- The tallest volcano in the solar system is on Mars.
- The islands of Hawaii are the tops of ocean volcanoes.

Io is slightly larger than Earth's moon and covered with hundreds of volcanoes.

23

Dangerous Volcanoes

Burning lava is not the only thing that makes a volcano dangerous. In countries such as Iceland, the heat melts snow and ice. This can cause floods. Eruptions also contain hot clouds of ash and poisonous gas. This makes the air dangerous to breathe. The clouds can bury homes in ash. The gas poisons trees and other plants.

How to Survive

When a volcano erupts you must act quickly.

- Close all windows and doors.
- Use goggles to cover your eyes.
- Secure a mask or damp cloth over your mouth and nose.
- Wear heat-resistant clothes.
- Leave the area as quickly as possible.
- Do not drive through an ash cloud.

Rescue workers helped survivors when Volcano Ontake erupted in Japan.

REAL LIFE

March 20, 2010

A volcano erupted in Iceland. By April 14, the ash cloud rose 35,000 feet into the air. It damaged airplane engines. Airline travel in Europe was stopped for seven days.

Job Profile

Scientists who study volcanoes are called volcanologists. Their jobs are dangerous. They measure a volcano's temperature and collect samples. They wear special protective clothing. The information they collect is used to predict when a volcano will erupt. It also helps scientists understand why eruptions happen.

Understanding Volcanoes

Many volcanoes are dormant. This means they are not erupting. But they could erupt in the future. Some volcanoes are extinct. This means they are not likely to erupt.

Bushfires

Why Do Bushfires Happen?

Bushfires start in hot, dry places. They are one of the most dangerous disasters. The most common place in which these fires occur is Australia.

Bushfires move quickly and burn everything in their path. The fires can be caused by many things. These include:

- lightning strikes
- people
- faulty electrical equipment

FIRE DANGER RATING TODAY

LOW-MODERATE · HIGH · VERY HIGH · SEVERE · EXTREME · CODE RED

PREPARE. ACT. SURVIVE

REAL LIFE

February 7, 2009
Bushfires burned through Victoria, Australia. Damaged equipment at a power plant started one fire. More than 3,500 firefighters rushed to the scene. More than 2,000 homes were destroyed, and 173 people died. It was named the Black Saturday Bushfire. It was one of the worst bushfires ever.

How Are Bushfires Stopped?

Strong winds help bushfires travel long distances. Bits of burning leaves and twigs can be carried by the wind. This starts more fires. Extreme temperatures can reach 2,220°F. The smoke contains poisonous gases.

Firefighters must work quickly to stop a bushfire. They dig trenches and clear trees that could become fuel. They spray water on the ground and the fire. Military pilots drop firefighting chemicals and water from the air.

Help Is at Hand!

Pets and wild animals need help in a disaster too. People take animals to special shelters. Shelter workers feed and care for them until it is safe.

These joeys in Melbourne, Australia, were lucky enough to be saved from a bushfire.

Glossary

black box	equipment that collects information
current	movement of water or air
humidity	amount of water in the air
lava	magma that flows out of a volcano
magma	liquid rock that is under the ground
molten	so hot that it has become liquid
porous	containing holes
pressure	force that can build up
trench	long, narrow hole dug in the ground
vent	gap through which things can escape

Index

animals 8, 12, 20, 31

ash clouds 24, 26

bushfires 28–31

electricians 15

firefighters 19, 29, 30

floods 10–15, 24

lava 22, 24

magma 22

meteorologists 6

poisonous gas 24, 30

rescue workers 8, 12, 19, 25

sinkholes 16–21

storm chasers 7

supercells 4

survival 8–9, 12–13, 24

thunderstorms 4

tornadoes 4–9

volcanoes 22–27

volcanologists 27

waterspouts 9

wind speeds 5, 6–7